Not Quite an Ocean
Elizabeth M. Castillo

Published by Nine Pens Press
2023
www.ninepens.co.uk

All rights reserved: no part of this book may be reproduced without the publisher's permission.
The right of the author to be identified as the author of this work has been asserted by them in accordance with the Copyright, Designs and Patents act 1988

ISBN: 978-1-7391517-4-4
018

Pacific

8   Welcome Friend
10 Rumours
11 Dig
14 Things that have replaced my Father
15 Teeth
16 Storm Tower
19 To be Woman

Atlantic

22 Waves
23 For Sarah, and all those whose names I'll never know
24 Poem after my four-year old's bedtime tantrum
25 When Mother Nature will not Wake
27 In Which Bertha Mason Cannot Sleep
28 Regret
29 Nereid

Arctic

32 20th December, *after Lucille Clifton*
33 The Other Woman
35 The Cancer
36 Origami
37 I am tired
38 The Sailor, the Pilgrim, and the Vagrant

Indian

40 In summer I am beautiful
41 Hymn of moss and consequence
42 Who will hold the ocean?
43 Love song
44 Body, i love you
45 What I like, *after Mary Ford Neal*

To Raphaëlle and Cassandre,
both nereids
and oceans
in their own right.

Pacific

Welcome, Friend

Before the girding of loins,

  before the great red of war, we rejoice to hold you

    captive, you, the captor   *(Welcome)*   See?

I trace your battle lines along my open palm Etch a mark

            for every hostage held. See?
            I have caught you like
            a hungry bear, her well-earned salmon

  Bathed myself in salt   *(you are welcome).*
                Laced your footprints with seeds

Come, I will hold a feast in your honour   *(welcome)*

    Cacao,
    manganese and
    cinnamon. Blood,
    sage and
    marrow

  Welcome, fire and earth, tonight will fly your colours   *(welcome)*

        See? The jade is prepared   Blades to cut,
                    to clear
                    (to welcome)   are at hand

I have marked your coming on a fishbone

I have felt it in the pull of the moon through the sea

I see it hanging off the shadow in my daughter's iris

    Welcome friend.

Your place is here with me.

Rumours

There's a rumour I've heard,
whistling through train tracks
pressed between feather pillows,
pushing up through cracks in the pavement.
Writhing, like eels. First this way,
then that.

For the most part, I've ignored it, poured myself
and my years into the circling of the earth, and the trees,
and their language. They murmur, you see, and it sounds like
the faint hum of a beehive.

It creaks and groans, like mountains stretching from tired *cimientos*.
Like the crash of the ocean against unyielding rock,
or the rumbling storm brewing in a horses' belly, before bolting.
Like the sting of silence above a desert's clavicle.
Whether whispered or cried, the words never falter.

There is no one. There's no one coming for you.

Dig

To write, dear lady, is to dig, is to
uncover. To dig and dig, until you swear
there cannot be anything more
beneath the topsoil, granite, even
beyond the water. Come with me;
I will show you how the roots are
fibrous here, like lace, like macrame,
dancing across the dirt. Frail in their
infancy, hopeful, reaching for creation,
for marriage, for descendants with
little lace shoots of their very own. See
how they race, tripping over themselves
for closure, catharsis. For just enough
light to make it home. Though they
seem fragile, I must warn you, they will
choke you without remorse. Best remain
upright, keep your wits about you in
the penumbra of this shifting soil.

>   Now we push past this chapter
>   to dig deeper. Hands, white-knuckled,
>   wielding the pick. There is blood here,
>   soaked into the dirt, dicot roots, thick,
>   reaching down into the earth, slashed
>   to pieces in many places. Some severed
>   completely from the plant that protrudes,
>   proud at the surface. See the faces etched
>   into the soil, forgotten. Hands and feet, and
>   hip bones. And ribs. There are lowly, vile
>   things hidden here, strangled by roots like

heavy ropes. The darkness of a year, of a
lifetime. Of learned behaviour. Of inadequate
speech. Of consequence. Of love, and knives,
and loss.

        Let's journey a little deeper, axe
in hand, sure to clear our down
-ward path. Be careful! There is
a void here, a great, cavernous hole,
retreating back into the soil. Here
there are no roots, just colours. Shades,
but never the right ones. There is
potential, but always it is wasted. There
is anger, terror, always dissolving into
lust. These are the lost years, the lost
roots. Too many languages to be
understood. Just stones, seeds,
boulders, and worms, untouchable
in their indifference. Do not tarry.
Neither you nor I are welcome here.

        The ground is pulsing, it's getting
warm. We're nearing the heat, the
heart of the thing. Here the roots
are heavy, and heaving, like
their buttress brothers above, and
rightly so. Anchors, if the earth were
an ocean, which it is, designed
to tether the sharpest corners
of your soul. Here you are,
little girl. Careless. Defiant. Chaos,
in tiny human form. And here,

tangled roots, unfurling from
fingernails,
like tendrils, twisting, like twine.
Enough force to gird your body; to
gird
the vast nebula of your mind. Here
the creeping speaks in electric
silence- a peal of laughter;
a mother's tired caress. There is room
here for affirmation, for repose.
For tenderness. There is strength
to be drawn from the centre, from
the
heart of earth itself. Here, remember,
and
have your fill of it. God knows you'll
be
needing every gritty
morsel
you
can

get.

Things that have replaced my Father

       Today.
The cult of oneself. Altars,
built at sporadic hours.
       Social media.
Poetry. Written in the bathtub, on my phone.
       Blood.
The defacing of my body. The misplacement of
lessons learnt.   Cause.
                       And consequence.
                       Reinvention
A sense of justice entirely my own. An
appetite for knowledge.   Paralysis.   Inertia.
A hunger for travel. A howling need to run.
Ungraciousness. Self-confidence.   Thunder.
The thrill of the hunt. The headlong pull of conquest.
My pathological inability to belong.
Men. At least four or five too many.
The burden of my people, whoever they are. Forgiveness.
Yes, sometimes even that can be wrong.
My father himself- his unfathomable approval.
And this dark cloud that I watch, helplessly, as it swallows him whole.

Teeth

She took out her teeth for love.
Dislocated her jaw, like a feeding constrictor.
Once queen of the forest, now glorified rope.
She took out her teeth for love, and her mouth was left gaping.
Blood pooled in the holes. The world tasted of iron.
She took out her teeth for love. Dismantled her mandibula.
Nursed the wounds as best she could.
There she sits now. At the junction of life.
Hungry. And toothless.

Storm Tower

The day is dark, as if coffee
spilled from your cup had stained atmosphere,
colouring the light dirt-grey. Something
is not as it should be. Everything
seems to pull to the east. There is a
warning in the air, as salt, suspended,
lingers above the sea. Words are
travelling to you, a message, swollen, begging
to be deciphered. One you can only hear in sleep.

Outside, you watch, transfixed, your thoughts
torn away from you, then regurgitated
back onto the shore. An endless cycle
of sand and water, and empty, bubbling foam. A sound,
a scent, pulls your gaze outwards. Something
gathers on the horizon- a thing you cannot see.
Something whistles at your back, but reaching around,
it slips, like satin between your fingers.
Far too quick to be caught in your grasp.

You keep your house empty, but the garden
full, though today the plants
seem to grovel and shake. They lie,
half-prone against the earth, heads
turned from the sun as it cowers behind the
clouds, in deference for whatever
comes in its wake. The sand beneath you
trembles, each grain sinking back down into
its brothers' horde. The waves retract- paying you
heed no longer, swallowing themselves
in their haste. They are never coming back.

Your blood, chilled, trickles inside you. Out there, you watch
the tower rise. Steps away from shelter, but
you're not sure your mind can trust what
your eyes are pleading with you to see. Sound
of pounding all around you. Beneath you.
Look down, you realise it is your own two
feet as you stumble backwards. Straining
for purchase on a door that is just out
of reach. Steady yourself. Gather your clothes
and wits about you. You can't outrun the storm.

Pressed up against the partition-
no match for what brews at its back. Sweat
meets ink, gathering at your wrist, your navel,
mottling the floor with drops of hopeless black. There is
nothing to be done. Nowhere to hide. It's far too late
for that. Except, perhaps, open the door? A rush
of madness courses through you, coating your mouth,
your palms. You've never courted a storm before.

The house is small, but solid, each wall built
just high enough. But from the east, through
panelling cracks, comes the battering
of wind, rhythmic- a beating of drums that have no care
for the water that they sift and throw up
with every roll and crash. Made wild, you feel them
in the ground beneath you, in the pulsing
in your own heart. These waves do not bend to any man.
You never stood a chance.

Your malformed mountains cannot protect you. No desert, no forest, can keep you safe. Straining against a keyhole barely wide enough to see through, there is no shelter in all this hollow place. Everything hangs in the balance of a moment. Your blood and your belly- they know what you must do. *Batten down the hatches. Board up the windows.* Wrap yourself in ash and sackcloth. You know the storm, she comes for you.

To be Woman

      is to be pieces
      is to be needed
      is to be blamed
      deserving at all times
To be Woman is not to be anything
      To be woman is to be everything
      All things bound together
      and, if you can manage it
      that little bit more
To be Woman
      is to be pitted
      teeth bared, taut muscle
      sharp claws, brawling
      raving, hungry
      backs against the wall
To be Woman
      is body dysfunction
      is body misunderstood
      is body underfunded, uninsured
      mystery illness, ovarian taxation
      reproductive discrimination
      persecution, enshrined in law
To be Woman
      is nurturing
      Provision
      is scheming
      Obsession
      Is wanton, waiting, abandon,
      a forest in an acorn,
      an ocean in a person

Atlantic

Waves

Have you ever stood inside the ocean?
Toes curled. Shaky purchase on the seafloor.
There is a lesson to be learned, if you will stand
and defy Poseidon inside his own court. Waves,
they travel single file. *To hide their numbers.*
Waves- they suffer neither fool nor survivor. Waves-
they just keep coming. The moon-
she has no care for the divisions of you life, for these
tiny boxes you amass and fill. Compartments overflowing,
still she stands, looming as her soldiers consider their
onslaught. Waves- breaking neither themselves nor each other.
Waves- at every side, there is no path outside of them. Waves-
exiling you back to the shore.

How long have you been standing here?

For Sarah, and all those whose names I'll never know

This isn't about poetry, so I won't make it about poetry.
This is about justice. About consequence. About rage.
I'm looking for a place to put all this anger.
Surely no page known to Man, certainly not to
Woman,
is big enough.
Sisters-in-arms, limp, sister-
dead in your arms. In your forests. Your ditches. Your cages.
Your home.

What do we have to do for you to stop killing us?

Strong,
black mothers raising families in America.
Mapuche
girls fighting for water, for land in the south.
Prisoners
of war, victims of the Congo saga.
Mauritian
wives, Mauritian daughters, cowering in their kitchens.
Desaparecidas, at Mexican borders, in Argentine towns.
A white girl,
an English girl, just walking home.

What do we have to do for you to stop killing us?

What have we done for you to hate us? Fed for centuries, yet still hungry
for blood. For milk. Sex. Hearth. The mothers, the sisters, the daughters.
The human beings- the living, breathing people. Invisible people.
Expendable people. Not *person* enough.

What do we have to do for you to stop killing us?

Poem after my four-year-old's bedtime tantrum

I just wanna / brush my teeth and cry in the dark / just wanna eat cheesy pasta / which is mostly cheese / just want my early wakeups to be hours before the alarm clock / want my lactose intolerance not to show up on my skin I / just wanna / hear your voice / rumble / against my ear / one last time / jus wanna / fold you back inside of me / safe / just wanna fill my house / with hanging plants / jus wanna forgive / forgive / forgive / as I am forgiven / just wanna / rent a car / drive through a snowstorm / want to / never have to come back here again / I just wanna fill / my lungs / with smoke / and hope / and ambition / just wanna let the grey grow out / live in a wood shack by the ocean / just wanna hear your voice / calling to me / once again / I just wanna make my peace and not / be your reason / for therapy / wanna stop forgetting to drink / my coffee / just wanna laugh / and love / and write / and make love / lose sight of / everything in between

When Mother Nature will not Wake

There is a girl here, she is a goddess and she is me.

There is a mountain beneath that girl, that heeds and kneels to the goddess, and that mountain is also me.

There are legs beneath that girl, as she stands, towering over, straddling that mountain.
Legs that reach beyond oceans, across seas. Legs that span the continents.

Beneath the mountain, Gaia[1] sleeps, weary from the angry years of men waging war across her skin, and plundering her depths with impunity. She sleeps because it is her time. Turning over in her slumber, she shifts the earth and its casing, throwing up the waters into one great wave, and splitting the ground beneath humanity in two.

In her rest she has sent her daughter in her stead, and her daughter is the girl.

There are waters inside this girl, rain and thunder that rage and roar. The sound of ravenous hunger not for food, but for blood, and conquest, and empire. And desire. She carries not her mother's weariness, and now she has awoken, she will no longer sleep. The storms inside drive this girl, this goddess, not to madness, but to understanding that is beyond the world of men. To her duty to the mother Durga[2], and to the earth she has left in her care. To gale-force winds, and feral, ferocious fire.

There is vengeance inside this girl, but she keeps it under lock and key. The key swings on a chain about the tall column of her neck- a warning to

---

[1] Mother Goddess of the earth according to Greek Mythology

[2] Hindu supreme Mother Goddess

those who might mistake her patience for weakness. There is greater strength in silence. In knowing one's weight and worth.

There are arms here, and hands. And fingers built for power, and possession. Built for conquest. The four winds heed their every flex, their every fold. Might, like a sword can be wielded both ways. But these hands course with creation, not destruction, sprouting cherry blossoms and fruiting trees in whichever direction they incline. Such is the divine way.

There are tears that fall here, over the equator. Over the Americas. Returning to the sea. There is pain that has been bartered, recycled into fodder, into food for the mountains and trees, as they too, awaken once more. The salt is gathered into the earth, and there sets itself, collects itself, as diamonds in the soil. Men will kill themselves, and each other for the tiniest sample of the goddess' sadness, the tears of the girl. Each year she will shed more.

There is patience here, marked as veins across her neck and wrists. Heavily they heave in her full breasts. Patience, and promise of provision, of providence. Of blessing and bounty and beauty, even in her great sadness. Blood and milk, surging through her. Bountiful harvest, just waiting to be birthed. She bears their weight gladly, knowing these are the means, and not the end.

There is a song here, a melody so terrible no ear can stand its sound. There are words sung in adoration, incantations, travelling upwards from the ground, from the very earth beneath her, the Pacha Mama[3] herself sings her own daughter's praises. Toasts her long-life, her great love, and her health.

---

[3] Amerindian Goddess of the Earth, or Mother Nature

In Which Bertha Mason Cannot Sleep

Look at you. Just look at you. Anxious.
Sweating. Crying over half a xanax that isn't
sending you over the edge in your cosy, 5-star
deluxe suite. Look at you plastering yourself in oils.
Repairing your skin barrier. Unclenching your jaw.

Look at you, in your great house your mother could
only ever have dreamed of. Look at you, quaking at the
fury of the ocean, as high tide tries to beat down your door.

Look at you, gaping like a catfish, knowing Rochester
was always the monster, and never you, all along.

Regret

shark   in the water
blood on   her fingers
blood on   the water
shark (death) on her   hands

Nereid

they say the Gods / in their love /
laced her mouth with nectar /
they say her mouth is a /
glorious / place
is / heaven / held taut
pleasure / honey pooling
on her tongue / her mouth is a / refuge
there is shelter there / they have
found home / in the hollow / of her cheeks
/ plump lips / pillowsoft / sharp
as thistle / sharp / as thorn / smiles / slashed
threat / beaming / her mouth
moves to spell the end / silt
and undertow / her mouth / is always open
welcoming the ocean / salt-lipped / coral-tongue
her mouth is a / love-song / suspended on
a spider's web / from the moon / to the shore
they say her mouth / is a place of / wonder /
those who go in / never ask for home / never return /
they say the gods / in their love /
laced her mouth with nectar / they forget / those very
same gods / also lined her mouth / with blade /
and bone / they forget / those very same gods / the ways of
men / and monsters / they forget / the gods / and men
that she is / always / hungry

Arctic

20th December
after Lucille Clifton

In a week I will be born
to the misplaced ambition of a woman
and a man whose feet would itch
to be anywhere but here. She will suture
me to her inner arm, there both a comfort
and a crutch, and he will censure me for it.
They will do for me and my brothers all that they can
but perhaps that is a lie.
we will plaster smiles across these infant years,
and she will live long, in spite of her best efforts.
in one week I will emerge, my small neck cordoned
and they will inhale their regret,
exhale their civil congratulations
and to their friends they will say
she is our pride and joy.

The Other Woman

The sun has set, and at this hour,
shadows hang between the daylight and the trees.
There, the sudden scent of blood,
                         scent of *man*,
carries to me on the breeze, the wind
howling through, falls silent at my feet:
                         "good hunting, milady,"
it whispers, then retreats. There is
a darkness in this forest, an end
that rivals death itself,
in the mist about my ankles. Even lizards
know they would do well to hide
inside their hovels, and underground.

Dirt crunches beneath.
                         Treacherous soil!
Leaves plunge downwards,
to be eaten by the earth.
The naked trees testify: this forest is deadly,
and will swallow you whole. I hear
footsteps racing, running, in thundering lockstep.
Flash of black. Flash of teeth.
                         There are dangerous games afoot!
Surely it's time to turn back. Surely it's time to go home.
I am well beyond my borders now.

She can't catch me, she can't catch me,
here, where I lurk
and linger on the periphery
just out of sight, just beyond her mind's eye.

She knows I am here, her veins
course with rage, and vengeance.
But she does not know where.
                                  She is death. She is danger.
But the line has been crossed,
the threat prowls within
her marked territory.
She may think I have lost,
but this no longer bears any resemblance to a fair
fight. No, now two legs, not enough.
I drop down onto four,
draw strength from the thousand invisible
heartbeats, the lifeblood,
the microbiome of the forest floor.

There is fear, and some fury,
encrusted under each hungry claw. The hunt
smells of my father, champion long before I
had ever heard of this sport, and I wonder:
                             would he be proud?
There is sweat at my temples, and my wrists are bound
to stop them from trembling.
I step, crabways, low and feral, without shadow
or sound. Your ears twitch and you shudder,
neck craning to see what you
and I must learn the hard way:

                                  the deadliest thing in here is me.

The Cancer

The earth was held between two breasts / warm
and safe from the beasts inside / the world
was kept against her chest / milk
from one / salt water from the other / the world
was split along her middle / one half wrenched /
like a joint / from a socket / like a feeding
calf / from its mother / the other
severed / long / painful / strokes / and she cried out /
this bleeding earth / with every motion / the faultlines
cracked / the oceans stood to attention / bursting their banks /
covering the earth / only volcanoes left standing /
spitting fire and ash / from their gaping
mouths / there was no alternative / it had to be done /
letting the blood / deep from the earth's core /
and after the rubble / after the rains / after much digging /
beneath each breast / that cradled the earth / lay the cancer /
they had buried there / long before

Origami

Fold myself up like an apology scribbled on a scrap of paper.
Like a receipt wrapped around a loose credit card you thought you'd lost.
Like a nervous thumb into a tight fist. A phone number, tucked into your back pocket.
Like the linens you forgot to hang out in time, and now stink of neglect.
Like your hand around a child's trusting palm.
Like a Paris restaurant, and its cloth napkins.
Like the end I have brought upon myself.
Like a delicate, paper swan.

I am tired

Bartering tomorrow's sanity for today's peace
Severing pieces of myself
Shrinking to fit into the spaces leftover
Occupying corners. Inhabiting peripheries. I am tired.

I am tired
Of armies I did not enlist in. Of wars I did not declare. Of quarrels
that don't exist. I am tired of
protestant productivity. Catholic guilt. Of crosses
I am unsure were ever mine to bear.

I am tired

But no one invites my head to rest on their shoulder.

I am tired.

But nobody puts me gently to bed.

The Sailor, the Pilgrim, and the Vagrant

I came across a mountain, or rather / a mountain crossed my path and it stood / unmoved / defiant / its foundations rumbling as it laughed / I took the mountain and ground it down / from summit to dicot root / ground it down to a hillside / to a hillock / to a heap / 'til it was nothing more than pebbles on the ground /

I came / I came across a river / like a pack of wildebeest / thundering across my path / in its rage it threw up / the silt and sediment of the river bank / and swollen, cleaved the earth / in two / I bent and took it all inside of me / swallowing until I felt the salt / rasp down my throat / the rest I sent along its way / and away it went / nursing its wounded pride /

I came across a forest / thick and humid / and hung with serpents / and smoke / a howling made its way to me / contracting to a whistle / weaving through the trees / I wound the mournful sound around my wrists / collected creatures in my pocket / and by means of starlight / set myself on fire / I burned the night forest down to ash / and ember / leaving nothing but a graveyard where it once stood /

I walked out of the darkness / and you crossed my path / neither dust / nor salt / nor ash had touched you / like nothing I / had ever seen / and in truth / I meant to simply keep on walking / but disaster / it seems / is tethered to my ankles / the road was long before me / I should have continued on my path / leaving you alone / leaving you behind / I should have gone on my way / I should have run / but

God help me,
(God help me!)
I didn't.

Indian

In summer I am beautiful

not like winter, when even the sun hides his face from me. As if the thought of spending the long, languid, dwindling of day in my company were too much to bear.

Winter where shadows creep and creep, where trees are naked, when hope decides to hibernate. In winter a greyness covers the earth– there's no telling the colour of a dandelion, or the green breadth of a blade of grass.

Like a faithful mouse I have learned to hoard small crumbs of happiness. The familiar creak in the floorboard. The last drop of tea left in the cup (for safekeeping). The steam-coaxed softness of skin.

Not so in summer.

In summer, I wear beauty like a shroud, and my solitude becomes a wildflower crown.

In summer, I gather beauty all about me:
wet at my temples / between my breasts / at the backs of my knees.

Like calls to like. Salt calls to salt.

There, submerged in the forgiving ocean, I find in water, and in summer, I am beautiful.

Hymn of moss and consequence

I wish for myself the luxury
of spreading across a
dark / forgotten corner of
the world / soft / like velveteen
moss / coating the underside
of a / fallen / tree / a giant
at rest / a home for
small / important creatures / I wish
to dangle / blissful / working
with / and not against / gravity's iron
pull / like ivy off a precipice / no
vertigo / not afraid to look
down / I wish to plunge
my roots deep into the
earth / trace my lineage / through
mantle / crust / and molten
core / to know the quiet strength
of mushrooms / to know fungi like
me are not so easily
moved / creep / goaded by the
sunlight / creep outwards / to fruit / and
flower / like lemon thyme / gather
myself into / a fragrant heap of
lavender / with the audacity of
bindweed / choke / the hope / from
every living thing / that dares / to cross
my path

Who will hold the ocean?

Who will comfort her in her rage?
Whose arms could wrap across the earth?
Whose legs wouldn't buckle under her constant motion?
Who could see past her belly swollen with oil and regret?
The great sutures that hold her together in her depths?
Who will breathe life into her wearied sinews, shore up the arms that hold the continents apart?
Who will tell her she is condemned to hunger?
Of the slander spoken by the rivers and streams?
Who will thank her for her giving, her constant giving?
Who will teach her that the darkest parts of her body are where creatures are the most boneless, and bright?
Who will dismantle the great, iron skeletons of conquest that lie rotting, eating away at her throat, and back teeth?
Who will whisper eulogies to her salt, to her sand?
Who will defy the moon, and the white tyranny he holds over her?
Who will hold up her glaciers, fractal by fractal, until she is spent?
Who will comfort the ocean?
Who will hold her ends in place?

Love song

I'm learning to fold myself into him, warm as he is.
My south to his north.
My mighty armies, his unbending will.
To trust myself in his arms, safe from the world (outside/inside).
To ask, and be given, is an art I've yet to master.
To take, and show gratitude, is no shameful task.
There's a strength in rupture, and a hope of new beginnings.
There's dignity in broken bones, and torn skin.
I've decided that I shall love him as I have never loved another.
I'm learning to listen: the gentle coax of a winter morning is his.
I'm learning to hear: the last whispered hope of the day is his.

Body, i love you

where you are. When you are. I am safe inside you, body. When you are a cellar. When you are a door. When you are a vehicle, like that second-hand citroen, with its littered floor, paint scratched from corners i didn't quite clear, from concrete barriers i never knew were there until it was too late.

Body, i love you. When you cling to walls like moss.
As a fruiting tree. As a crack in the glass.
Wolf-proud. Urchin-shy.

Body, forgive me, for hardening my ear against you. For dismissing your aching cries, your silent grieving. Always so busy folding you up, busy tucking you in– *body, body* you are marvellous!

See how filth washes right off of you, how none of it ever really touched you– see, if i tilt my head, you are still upright– *body*, you're no thing to be hidden, *body*, i know you are mostly salt and water. You are your very own equator. You were meant for the sun.

I've been a fool, *body*, forgive me. Hemmed discontent into each of your sinews. Tucked the world and its worries in between each vertebrae. Filled your liver with anguish. Let your uterus fester with regret.

Body, i believe you. I believe you. Heart– take my allegiance. Feet– i will turn you loose onto the ground you long to feel beneath you. Eyes– i will follow you. Obedient, like a lamb.

Body, i love you. I set love aside for you. You are safe inside me, *body*. When you are. Where you are.

Body, i love you.

What I like
after Mary Ford Neal

Tell me what you like, she says,
eyes wide, mouth in earnest.
Tell me what you like,
her voice trembling with youth,
and confidence wholly her own.
Pressed against me, yet there are
entire oceans between us.
Very well. I'll tell you what I like.

I like myself. I like who I am.
I like the books I read and the rhythm of my choices.
I like my mind, the ideas that form and flutter,
when I'm in bed, or in the bath. I like the
kindness I have wrought, especially when the recipient
was undeserving. I like the fullness of my hips
and the softness of my belly, and the way
my shadow waxes and wanes with the tide.
I don't like all my mistakes, but I like
what I have learned from them.
I like my gold jewellery, and my octopus wall art.
I like my face, and my humour. My hand,
when it's laced together with my husband's,
and my voice, when it's coaxing calm into the
heart of a child. I like my understanding
of the world, and my way with plants, and people.
I like my freckles, and my brown skin, especially when I'm underwater.
I like speaking my languages.

I like who I have become.
I like who you will become.

Acknowledgments

I would like to thank all the journals and magazines that have published individual poems from this collection, namely *Yellow Arrow Journal* (Welcome, Friend), *Epoch Press* (Dig), *Fiery Scribe Journal* (Storm Tower), *Fahmidan Journal* (When Mother Nature Will Not Wake), *The Elpis Pages*, and the *Bournemouth Fresher Writing Prize* (The Other Woman). Thank you for believing in my words, I would not have found my readers without your support.

To Colin and the Nine Pens team, for reaching out and giving my work such a wonderful home, and everything they are doing for the indie publishing world. It's an absolute honour to be working with you. I am also very grateful to all those who provided editorial feedback on individual poems: Nikki, Tyler, Keshe, Maria, Alex, Glenn, Louise, SG, Beth, Gavin, Nick, Antony, Lisa, Jen. You are rock stars and I love you!

I would like to thank my Father, who gave me words and any talent I might have to wield them. In all my ways I acknowledge you.

A big thank you to my parents who taught me to love poetry and pursue my dreams; my phenomenal (woman) sister who always encouraged my writing; my imaginary friend Caroline who threw me headfirst into taking my writing seriously. Also to my beautiful Pongs, Pops, Fatty 1, and Fatty 2 who are always ready to celebrate me and my creative pursuits.

I would not be writing poetry, or writing at all if it weren't for the support of the amazing writing friends I have made along this journey, particularly Laura, Nikki, Jen, Martha, Lisa A, Lisa M, Sarah, Shiksha, Antony, SG, Niall, Nick, Robin, Andres, Alba, Keshe, Andrei, Ben, Kellasandra, Miguel, Ricardo, and many more. Writing can be a lonely business, and it's been nothing short of a privilege to have you on my path so far.

I owe a great deal of thanks to Sarah Everard, Penelope Bianca Adès, Charlotte Brontë, Madeleine Miller, Lucille Clifton, and Mary Ford Neal, who each directly inspired a poem in this short collection.

And lastly I'd like to thank the ocean, and all its creatures, as well as women everywhere.

www.ingramcontent.com/pod-product-compliance
Lightning Source LLC
Chambersburg PA
CBHW021134080526
44587CB00012B/1282